The Gam

CW00996641

Nelson

Mother went to Picnic Wood
to look for some coconuts.

She found
three coconuts.

When she came back Trog said,
'Did you find some coconuts?'
'Yes,' said Mother.
'I found three coconuts.'
'There is me and there is you,'
said Trog.
'There is Father and there is Grandpa.
That makes four of us,
but we only have three coconuts.'

'We shall play a game,' said Mother.
'We shall see who is going to have
the coconuts.
We shall play *ibble*, *obble*,
black, *bobble*, *ibble*, *obble*, *OUT*.'
'How do you play that?' said Trog.

'We must sit down,' said Mother.
'We must sit down in a ring.'
Mother said *ibble* to herself,
obble to Father,
black to Trog,
bobble to Grandpa,
ibble to herself,
obble to Father,
and *OUT* to Trog.

'Trog is out,' said Mother.
'Grandpa has a coconut,
Father has one,
I have one but Trog will not have one.
He can have some of mine.'
'That is a good game,' said Grandpa.
'I have a coconut.'

Father went to Picnic Wood
to look for some bananas.
He found three bananas.

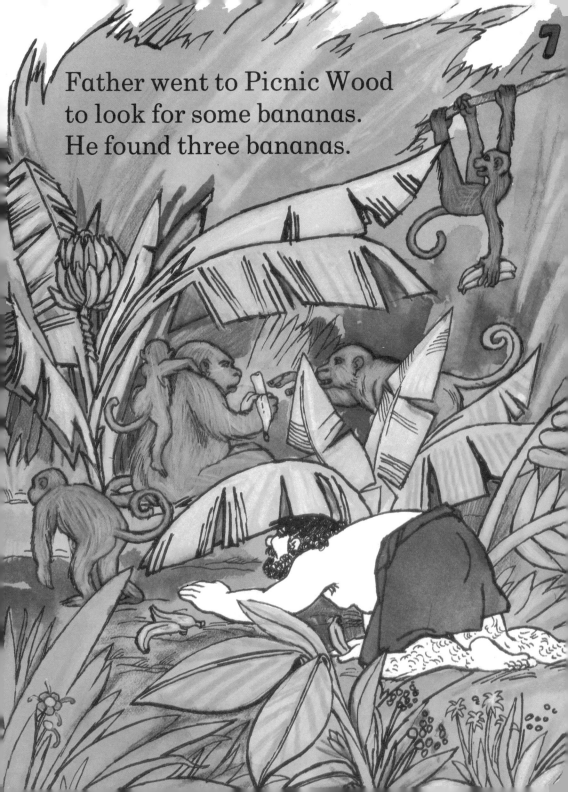

When he came back Trog said,
'Did you find some bananas?'
'Yes,' said Father.
'I found three bananas.'
'There is me and there is you,'
said Trog.
'There is Mother and there is Grandpa.
That makes four of us,
but we only have three bananas.'

'We shall play that game,' said Grandpa.
'We must sit down in a ring.'
Mother said *ibble* to Father,
obble to Trog, **black** to Grandpa,
bobble to herself,

ibble to Father,
obble to Trog,

and **OUT** to Grandpa.

'Er, no, I didn't mean
that game,' said Grandpa.
'I meant ***Ip dip doo,
cat's got flu,
dog's got chickenpox,
out go YOU***!'
'Very well,' said Mother.
'We shall play Grandpa's game.'

Grandpa said *Ip* to Mother,
dip to himself,
doo to Trog,
cat's to Father,
got to Mother,
flu to himself,

dog's to Trog,
got to Father,
chickenpox to Mother,
out to himself,
go to Trog, and *YOU*! to Father.
'Father is out,' said Mother.
'Grandpa has a banana,
Trog has one,
I have one but Father
will not have one.
He can have some of mine.'
'That is a good game,' said Grandpa.
'I have a banana.'

Grandpa went to Picnic Wood.
He found three eggs.
'I found three eggs,' said Grandpa.
'We shall play that game.
We must sit in a ring.'

Grandpa said
Ip to Father, *dip* to Mother,
doo to Trog, *cat's* to himself,
got to Father, *flu* to Mother,
dog's to Trog, *got* to himself,
chickenpox to Father,
out to Mother, *go* to Trog,
and *YOU*! to himself.

'Out? ME!' shouted Grandpa.
'Er, no, I didn't mean that game.
I meant **Eeny**, **Meeny**, **Miney**, **Mo**...'